MY
REALITY CHECK

BOUNCED

**Confessions of a
Twenty-First-Century
Sinner**

RANDI KONIKOFF,
NCC, LPCS, CCS, LCAS

WESTBOW
PRESS®
A DIVISION OF THOMAS NELSON
& ZONDERVAN

Scripture taken from the Holy Bible, NEW INTERNATIONAL VERSION®.
Copyright © 1973, 1978, 1984, 2011 by Biblica, Inc. All rights reserved worldwide.
Used by permission. NEW INTERNATIONAL VERSION® and NIV® are
registered trademarks of Biblica, Inc. Use of either trademark for the offering
of goods or services requires the prior written consent of Biblica US, Inc.

Scripture quotations are from The Message. Copyright © by
Eugene H. Peterson 1993, 1994, 1995, 1996, 2000, 2001, 2002.
Used by permission of NavPress Publishing Group.

Scripture quotations are from The Holy Bible, English Standard Version®
(ESV®), copyright © 2001 by Crossway, a publishing ministry of
Good News Publishers. Used by permission. All rights reserved.

WestBow Press books may be ordered through booksellers or by contacting:

WestBow Press
A Division of Thomas Nelson & Zondervan
1663 Liberty Drive
Bloomington, IN 47403
www.westbowpress.com
1 (866) 928-1240

ISBN: 978-1-5127-0799-1 (sc)
ISBN: 978-1-5127-0801-1 (hc)
ISBN: 978-1-5127-0800-4 (e)

Library of Congress Control Number: 2015913809

Print information available on the last page.

WestBow Press rev. date: 09/21/2015

To my Savior, Jesus Christ

My children, Chavaleh, Emerald, and Elijah

My son-in-law, Brian

My siblings, Mark, Ross, and Barbara

"Randi has a hard time."

-Frances Konikoff, October 1, 1974

Contents

OVERTURE

I struggle. I've always been on the outside; never felt like I fit in. That's probably why being on stage in the spotlight felt so comfortable. I didn't have to fit in. I was set apart on purpose, so it was okay. I came from a show business family, and we were all gifted in our own special way. Being on stage and performing was as natural to us as breathing. There was no ego or star persona associated with it. It was what Daddy did for a living, so we always looked at it as our job—some go off to work at an office, and we went off to work at the theatre, the club, and the studio.

My days in show business were limited, but my career in the music industry yielded studio work, tours, shows, five CDs and hundreds of songs. But God had something else He wanted me to do. I was becoming too attached and identifying myself too much with my music. He moved me away from that, and I had no choice but to leave it, but I went kicking and screaming. Remember, I struggle.

He put me to work in an entirely different capacity. When God wants you to do something, He gets you ready and gets you going. He's not deterred by a little kicking and screaming. I remember when we were training our puppy, the trainer told us to periodically roll him on his back and gently, but firmly, hold him there. It is a process they call "submission." I can relate, puppy.

So, this is for the ones who struggle, the ones who have always felt they were on the outside. Even churches don't always get us. I didn't grow up *in the church*, so I don't always look or say things like everyone else. But Jesus gets me, and He gets you. He made us who we are, and He thinks enough of us to die for us. So, celebrate who you are by magnifying the one who made you for His glory.

For we are God's handiwork, created in Christ Jesus to do
good works, which God prepared in advance for us to do.
—Ephesians 2:10 NIV

Every breath you take

When my brother got electrocuted, fell forty feet off a ladder and landed headfirst on a marble floor, he was placed on a mercy flight to the hospital. All this took place before the family even knew what had happened. His wife, a nurse practitioner, called me first to start the family notification chain.

This was before the days of cell phones, so I had to go through the travel agency to help me track down my parents, who were on vacation five thousand miles away. I then called my other brother and sister.

And we prayed. We prayed in steps and stages. The first prayer was for my brother to live. God, please keep my brother alive. He went through many brain surgeries to reduce fluid buildup and reattach vital connections. God answered that prayer, and he kept breathing. He was alive. Thank you, Lord.

And we prayed. Now we prayed for brain activity and for God to bring him out of the coma. God answered that prayer, and there was brain activity, and he opened his eyes. Thank you, Lord.

And we prayed. We prayed for him to still be my brother—for him to still be himself. Time passed, and he spoke, and we all cried because God had answered our prayers. Thank you, Lord.

We knew God had given us a great blessing. The road since then has been rocky, with seizures, restrictions, and life adjustments. However, my brother is still breathing, still sharing his personality and his life with us, and we are so grateful.

Each breath is a gift. Not just the breath that comes after a prayer to sustain the life of a loved one. The several breaths you have taken while reading this are just as precious and just as much a gift as those given to my brother in those prayer-filled days following his accident. From the first breath given to Adam out of the very mouth of God (Genesis 2:7 NIV), to God-breathed Scripture (2 Timothy 3:16 NIV), to our Savior Jesus, who breathed his last breath on the cross (Mark 15:37 NIV), we are reminded of its importance.

The Spirit of God has made me; the breath
of the Almighty gives me life.
—Job 33:4 NIV

JOY

Our creator has instilled in our brain the marvelous ability to experience joy. It's built into our brain chemistry. Start by thinking of your five senses: listening to beautiful music, tasting a good meal, feeling the sun warming your skin, smelling the scent of your favorite flower, or watching a sunset. Then add other joy producers: being with special friends, accomplishing something you have worked hard for, and the all-time bases-loaded-home-run feeling from requited love! Unless you have hijacked your brain's joy regulator through substance use, this gift of joy is queued up and ready to go. Let's say you have messed around with your brain chemistry. I have worked with many recovering addicts who, through time in treatment, have experienced the brain's amazing capacity to recalibrate itself. There's nothing healthier than a natural high. Joy.

You were taught, with regard to your former way of life, to put off your old self, which is being corrupted by its deceitful desires; to be made new in the attitude of your minds.
—Ephesians 4:22–23 NIV

WRECK LESS ABANDON

God calls us to recklessly abandon ourselves to him. Oswald Chambers writes, "You will only realize His voice more clearly by recklessness" (Chambers, 1935). I started thinking about this. What is the opposite of reckless? May I suggest that the opposite of living recklessly for God is living reckfully for ourselves? Now, let's tweak the spelling to add meaning—wreckfully. It has been proven in my own life that failure to live recklessly for God is living wreckfully for myself. God has shown me time and time again that I wreck less when I follow Him! There have been many times when I hesitated to act on a strong feeling or an opportunity, allowing anxiety, fear, and second-guessing to keep me from being a part of something amazing for God. He doesn't need our help, but He invites us to share in the wonder of His works. So listen up, tune in, cast off all wreckfullness, and abandon yourself recklessly to a life filled with opportunity and adventure! Now that's a life worth living.

And God is able to bless you abundantly, so that in all things
at all times, having all that you need, you will abound in every
good work. As it is written: "They have freely scattered their
gifts to the poor; their righteousness endures forever." Now
he who supplies seed to the sower and bread for food will
also supply and increase your store of seed and will enlarge
the harvest of your righteousness. You will be enriched in
every way so that you can be generous on every occasion, and
through us your generosity will result in thanksgiving to God.
—2 Corinthians 9:8–11 NIV

Your work is not your worth

On Wednesday you were let go from your job, due to budget cuts. You are devastated, as you gave everything you had to that job. Wait. Before you take the emotional express bus to the corner of Worthless Way and Loser Lane, let me invite you to Reality Road. Your value as a person is the same on Wednesday, after receiving that news, as it was on Tuesday, before you received that news. You did not change; your situation changed. You do not have to let a situational change affect who you are. Your work is not your worth. You do not have value because of what you do or what you have achieved. You have value because you are—because you exist. God created you because He wanted the world to have a *you* in it. He hand-picked everything about you. When you find yourself letting the world define who you are, look to Him instead. No one knows your value and your worth better than the one who made you.

For God so loved the world, that he gave his only Son, that whoever believes in him should not perish but have eternal life.
—John 3:16 ESV

Back-to-school shopping

Back-to-school shopping, four life-threatening words!
Isn't a notebook a notebook? "No, that one's for nerds!"

Here are the pencils. "Mom, no one uses those!"
They had something to say about each item I chose!

Okay, here's my card—get only what you need.
Two shopping carts later, I'm feeling fatigued!

I come from an era when back to school meant
One pair of shoes, one pair of sneakers.
Now, those cost one month's rent!

Tablets and binders and Sharpies and pens.
Ball point or gel grip, get hip to the trends!
Folders and locker shelves and butt-wipes gone wild!
Choosing a backpack is like adopting a child!

I love all my kids and will soon miss these days.
My blessings abound in the midst of this haze.

My oldest, my rock, stands by me and smiles.
"Remember the days when we walked these aisles?"
She's right. In a flash, twenty years have gone by.
I hug her so tightly and wipe a tear from my eye.

In less than four years, I'll be sitting at home
While others rush around and lament with a poem.

Thank you, Lord, for each moment. Your provision is sure.
Whether school supplies or life supplies, my soul is secure.

And my God will meet all your needs according
to the riches of his glory in Christ Jesus.
—Philippians 4:19 NIV

Even therapists get the blues

... and dentists get cavities, cartographers make U-turns, and a genius can forget where she put her keys. Robert Palmer sang, "You like to think that you're immune to the stuff, oh yeah." We are all unique, but there are some aspects in which we are very much the same. I can remember going through an emotionally rough patch for a few weeks. I tried to keep up the same pace, the same face. My self-talk consisted of little jabs and reminders that I should know better than to succumb to falling into the depressive abyss. Can you identify with that tactic? When you're not performing well or feeling up to par, do you engage in ridicule and chastisement in an attempt to fan your ember into a flame? Do you do this to your spouse or your kids? It rarely works. A seed of bitterness can grow from without or from within.

Albert Ellis, who is identified with Rational Emotive Behavioral Therapy, coined a wonderful expression. He said that if you are in the habit of telling yourself you should do this and you should do that, or you should not have done this or that, then you need to stop should-ing on yourself! And that's just what it feels like!

So, therapist, heal thyself? Well, sort of. When I finally got sick and tired of feeling sick and tired or, as the Bible refers to it, when I came to my senses, I employed techniques that have helped quite a few of my clients, and I also sought the help of a fellow therapist. After successfully moving up, up, and out of that pit, I remarked in surprise, "Wow, this stuff really works!" Having experience now on both sides of the clinical couch, I can recommend with confidence that seeking professional services for a repair, a tune-up, or an overhaul is a wise and beneficial decision.

Take words with you and return to the Lord. Say to
him: "Forgive all our sins and receive us graciously,
that we may offer the fruit of our lips."
—Hosea 14:2 NIV

Pause for paws

I'm dog sitting this week. Eva is a very sweet rescue dog with severe attachment disorder. Perhaps that's why my friends asked me to pet sit for them. Eva is not content with just sitting near you or beside you. Eva must be sitting on you. If it was possible, I believe she would hold you down with her paws. Instead, she holds you down with her most powerful weapon—her eyes. Oh, those eyes: two big, black pools of bottomless longing. There is such fear in there. During a recent thunderstorm, she actually crawled into the dryer and hid among the warm sheets and towels. Eva needs. She needs security, safety, attention, affection, comfort, and kindness. She, like all of us, was made with the capacity to give love and the desire to be cared for. Our fears may not drive us to crawl into the dryer, but they do drive us, nonetheless. We aren't as transparent as dogs, who can't help but show their emotions through that wagging tail: their barometer of happiness. You know just where you stand with a dog. We, however, have developed the art of pretense. We value it so much that we actually refer to it as an art. You can be talking to me face-to-face and I may be as smooth as glass on the outside, but on the inside I am a raging storm. Once Eva settles down on my lap, I let her stay there and notice that in a few minutes her breathing slows down, and she rests her head on my knees. Calm washes over her. That's how it feels to come to the Lord and rest in Him. When I come into His presence, with my heart racing in fear and my mind overloaded with worry, I feel calm wash over me. I feel security, safety, attention, affection, comfort, and kindness. I am safe in Him.

Cast all your anxiety on him, because he cares for you.
—1 Peter 5:7 NIV

Halloween flashbacks

I've been a Mom for thirty-five years. Halloween has changed a lot over that time. I can't remember every single one, but a few come to mind. The year we all had the flu and thoughtlessly handed out candy at the door, infecting all unsuspecting trick-or-treaters. Or the year I decided my oldest was going as Mr. Peanut, and I spent all day trying to figure out how a ten-year-old would be able to sustain holding a monocle in her eye all night. Then there was the year we worked so hard on painting the sandwich board she wore as the Queen of Hearts only to discover she couldn't get her hands around the board to hold her pillowcase out for candy. So much energy expended to run around in the dark. Halloween night in Buffalo usually meant wearing your winter coat over your costume, anyway. This Halloween, my oldest daughter is on a cruise with her husband; my middle daughter is at a high school football game; and my son and his friend are baking peanut butter cupcakes and playing Just Dance on the X-Box. The neighbors are blasting "Let's Do the Time Warp Again," and I hand out foil-wrapped chocolate body parts at the door, watching younger moms and dads make memories with their little princesses, superheroes, monsters, and cartoon characters. And so goes another Halloween.

There is a time for everything, and a season
for every activity under the heavens.
—Ecclesiastes 3:1 NIV

Under done

I don't know if it was the Christmas spirit, the Christian radio station, or the Holy Spirit (would be my pick), but I was moved this morning to send each of my three children a text message telling them how much I love them and how much they mean to me. I was compelled to let them know, and it felt really good. I also felt great joy at the idea that this text may brighten their day. Almost immediately, and almost simultaneously, I heard my iPhone chime with responses from all three. Eager to read their texts, I was both amused and humbled to read that not one, not two, but all three responses were the same. "Mom, what's wrong?" This is what I get for spontaneously declaring my love for my children—something must be wrong? Ouch. Could the message be any clearer? I need to do this more often. They need to hear it more often. So, to all of you who God has brought into my life, I am so grateful for your friendship, your accountability, your sharpness, and your grace. And no, there is nothing wrong!

...making the most of every opportunity,
because the days are evil.
—Ephesians 5:16 NIV

Appearing daily

Every day, if you choose to, you are invited to attend the most spectacular light show that has ever been produced. Each performance is unique; there is no reserved seating; the venue is never sold out; the cost is completely free. There are two shows offered daily, so if you miss the early show you can always catch the late one. The show's producer is an altruistic benefactor, desiring to demonstrate His authority over all nature by donating His talents simply for pure enjoyment. He invites us to begin our day with glorious beauty and prepares us for nightly rest with a similar display in breathtaking proportion—as if to reassure, "Have no fear, I am here in the morning and I am here in the evening." Occasionally, He provides a preview of His artistic expertise on His massive sky canvas in the form of a multi-hued rainbow—another reminder of His blessed assurance. If you have ever accepted His invitation and attended one of His shows, you could give a testimony to the awe and humility you experienced. There is nothing you were asked to do, nor could have done, to cause, prevent, or augment this display of His splendor. It is a gift, which we are asked only to receive.

The heavens declare the glory of God; the
skies proclaim the work of his hands.
—Psalm 19:1 NIV

A GOOD MORNING

I made breakfast for the family this morning. Did you feel the earth move? Chocolate chip pancakes, and not the kind you put in the toaster! I felt so fulfilled. And hold off judging me on the nutritional value. It sure beats yesterday's breakfast of onion dip and potato chips. Allow me to bask in five minutes of glory. I lovingly plated the stacks and watched with great pride as my children tore into them, nodding in silent approval. I will always cherish the words of my son as he took his last bite. "Mom, these are actually good!" Sweeter than syrup to my ears.

Her children arise and call her blessed ...
—Proverbs 31:28a NIV

Tick tock

I find myself with an extra half hour. I didn't know about it ahead of time, or I would have filled it faster than Usain Bolt! Is there such a thing as extra time? Isn't that like trying to catch up on sleep? You can't bank time, and you can't earn more. You get what you get!

So, if it's not how much we get, then it must be what we *do* with it that determines its value. We acknowledge that it is a commodity, but we can't buy it or sell it. We can't stop it or change its pace. We can only use it. Its value is relative. Does eight hours of playing a video game equate to eight hours of composing a symphony? Does one year in the life of a toddler have as much value as the last year of an octogenarian's life?

We are all given time. How much are we allotted? Most of us would say, "Never enough." The creator of time disagrees. He says we are given just enough, and what we do with it matters. Lord, help me to redeem the time you have given me in a way that honors you.

You saw me before I was born and scheduled each day of my life before I began to breathe. Every day was recorded in your book!
—Psalm 139:16 TLB

Tell me what's going on GOD? How long do
I have to live? Give me the bad news!
—Psalm 39:4 MSG

Teach us to number our days, that we
may gain a heart of wisdom.
—Psalm 90:12 NIV

… for we were born but yesterday and know nothing,
because our days on earth are a shadow.
—Job 8:9 MEV

Show me, LORD, my life's end and the number of
my days; let me know how fleeting my life is.
—Psalm 39:4 NIV

WHEN YOU'RE HOT, YOU'RE HOT - WHEN YOU'RE NOT, YOU'RE EATING OUT

First and foremost, I am not a cook. If you read my blog, you know this already. However, I have been seeing all these inventive and inspiring recipes for making healthy food. I got so excited! I thought, I can do this! I should have remembered my kid's response every time I attempted to make food in the past—"Oh no, Mom. Where are we going for dinner?" Brutal …

Tonight, I was moved to create something fantastic! I went at it like a crazed Renoir, madly sprinkling grated parmesan over hot steamed broccoli with visions of melted magnificence. Then I placed pre-warmed slices of turkey, ever-so-aesthetically over the cheesy crowns. My finishing touch was delicately rolling it all up in a soft burrito. It was awful. "Where are we going for dinner?" is coming from the back of the house. My son actually has the car keys in hand. What I lack in culinary skill, I make up for with enthusiasm! Unfortunately, that doesn't fill the tummy.

I was young and now I am old, yet I have never seen the
righteous forsaken or their children begging bread.
—Psalm 37:25 NIV

I GOTTA BE ME

I do not "work out." I will not "work out." Ex-Jewish American Princesses do not sweat. We mist. From what I understand, working out involves sweating. Lots of sweating.

I also try to avoid discomfort at all costs. I'm still looking to hire someone who will exercise for me. Hey, we pay people to walk our dogs, mow our lawns, and shop for our food—is this too much of a stretch (pun intended)? It could be a new twist on the personal trainer. Text your workout routine to your PT and have him text you back when he's done! Ah, feel the virtual burn!

They tell me to find something I enjoy doing and "just do it." I enjoy sitting and eating. My plan is to do three reps of this a day and work up to five or six.

Do you not know that your bodies are temples of the Holy Spirit, who is in you, whom you have received from God? You are not your own; you were bought at a price. Therefore honor God with your bodies.
—1 Corinthians 6:19–20 NIV

To LOVE

If you are sitting alone this Valentine's Day, or you are involved in a relationship where you feel alone, do something incredibly healthy for yourself. Go to the store and pick out a beautiful rose and a box of chocolates. Now give them to someone else. Brain science has proven that the pleasure experienced from doing something for another lasts longer and is felt more deeply than any self-directed act.

Do you have any idea of how much you are loved? Not because of what you do or what you have done, but just because you are? Your value and worth are not measured by how many valentines you got at school or by how quickly you were picked for kickball. They are also not measured by the failure of a parent to build or sustain a relationship with you.

My heavenly Father directs us *to* love—not to go out and seek love, or look for love, or earn love. But *to* love. And that includes loving ourselves. It's a curious thing. If everyone would just start *giving* love, we'd all be saturated in love. You don't reach a love limit. Just ask my friends with seven kids!

We have the example of utmost love—love for our highest good, a sacrifice of love beyond measure. Whether you believe you deserve it or not, whether you believe in Him or not, He still loves you.

But God demonstrates His own love for us in this:
While we were still sinners, Christ died for us all.
—Romans 5:8 NIV

Blood is thicker than slaughter

In the 1960s I was a little girl growing up in a Jewish family in a suburb of Buffalo, New York, I remember a man named Jerry Starr. Mr. Starr was well-known in the community. I remember him because every year he would volunteer to work any job on Christmas Eve or Christmas Day, so that those celebrating the holiday would be able to spend it with their families. And people took him up on it. It was just something he did. And it is still a beautiful example of putting someone else's needs above your own.

Now, lest you think it was a fairytale life we led, far from it. Anti-Semitism was alive and well back then, and we faced our share. Daddy was famous, well respected, and that may have spared us on occasion, but we were treated differently.

I have always been very proud of my Jewish heritage and even more proud to be a member of my wonderful family. At thirty-six years old, I came to the understanding that Jesus Christ died for my sins. So compelling and life-changing was this truth that my life has not been the same since. I deeply love and identify with my blood relatives, and I also deeply love and identify with my adopted Christian brothers and sisters. We both share the same G_d.

I do not understand everything, but I do know that I choose to stand shoulder to shoulder with my family lineage, to fight this most evil and present danger barreling down upon us. Can we take our queue from Mr. Starr and come alongside our brothers and sisters to offer support and solidarity? This is not a time for division but for rock-solid strength.

A new command I give you: Love one another. As I have loved you, so you must love one another. By this everyone will know that you are my disciples, if you love one another. —John 13:34–35 NIV

Tail chasing

We yearn so deeply to be accepted for who we are but strive without ceasing to become who we are not. Wow! That's not even the futility of chasing our own tail. That's chasing someone else's!

There is freedom in acceptance: the freedom to rest and the freedom to let go. There is freedom in letting others choose to behave in ways that may even appall us. Freedom without feeling compelled to correct them or become entangled in emotional angst over how wrong we think they are! Develop and practice acceptance of ourselves and acceptance that others are who they are. What a burden is then lifted off your back!

Do not assume I am suggesting you accept mistreatment, bad habits in yourself, and mediocrity. There is a difference.

However, what we resist persists. If all our focus is on resisting what we won't accept, we are not free to move forward. Consider accepting what *is* and disengaging from the frustration of resistance. Channel your efforts into removing yourself from toxic relationships, into giving grace to those who are struggling, and into letting go of a need to receive from others what only God can give to you.

For in Christ all the fullness of the Deity lives in bodily
form, and in Christ you have been brought to fullness.
He is the head over every power and authority.
—Colossians 2:9–10 NIV

Keep the light on

A steady power source keeps the light bulb shining strong, without flickering. When the connection is disturbed, the light dims, loses consistency, and eventually provides no light whatsoever. Have you had a short in your power source? Are you starting to believe who the world says you are rather than who you were created to be? Is your light flickering? Has it already gone out? Plug in to the Light.

God is light; in him there is no darkness at all.
—1 John 1:5b. NIV

THE OLD, GRAY MARE

My kids get a kick out of playing a game they call, "Who's older than Mom?" I don't get no respect. The other night the comparison group was NASCAR drivers. After much hilarity, as they ruled out driver after driver, it was determined that the only living driver older than Mom is Richard Petty. With all respect to The King, that stung.

My son thinks it's funny when using the self-checkout at the grocery store, to loudly ask me if I want the senior citizen discount today. Not yet, son, not yet.

I don't think I'm ready for the early bird special at Denny's or Mah Jong just yet, but I have lived an amazingly full life. I wish I hadn't made some of the choices I made, but the consequences, insights, and God's grace have made me who I am today—a bit younger than Mr. Petty and a lot wiser than I used to be.

Even when I am old and gray, do not forsake me, my
God, till I declare your power to the next generation,
your mighty acts to all who are to come.
—Psalm 71:18 NIV

The way

What you see as hate, I see as love.

If you and I are walking up a mountain and I see you take a trail that I believe will lead you to your death, I am going to share that information with you. I see that as an act of love, not hate! You always have the choice to heed my warning and choose another way or to continue on the path you have chosen. But the most loving action I can take is to let you know that I believe there is danger ahead for you.

This would be especially true if I had taken that other path myself, years earlier, and experienced the terrain and the terrible consequences. The way I see it, it would be hateful for me to refuse to warn you! It is out of love that I share this with you and risk your taking offense.

Whether you turn to the right or to the left, your ears will hear a voice behind you saying, "This is the way; walk in it."
—Isaiah 30:21 NIV

GOD HITS YA, HALLELUJAH!

My family has experienced a miracle: an "immeasurably more than all we ask or imagine" miracle. There is absolutely no doubt that it is God's divine intervention. It is beyond our wildest dreams. It is entirely undeserved, and it completely confirms His direction for our lives. God not only showed up, He showed out!

Why are we, as believers in Jesus Christ, so amazed when He delivers on what He promises? He is our Father; He cannot lie; His Word is faithful; and He will never leave us or forsake us. While I know I need never doubt His Word, I don't think I ever want to stop being amazed by Him! Who are we that He should provide such personal answers to our prayers and be so involved in every detail of our lives?

I do not understand a love like this. It's not just an abundantly generous love, it is also an overwhelmingly compassionate love, displayed through His comforting presence as He holds us and helps us survive the worst of times.

My Savior, my Lord, my prayer is to forever be in awe of you. Thank you. Thank you. Thank you.

Now to him who is able to do immeasurably more than all
we ask or imagine, according to his power that is at work
within us, to him be glory in the church and in Christ Jesus
throughout all generations, for ever and ever! Amen.
—Ephesians 3:20–21 NIV

THERE IS A GOD IN ISRAEL

After a mountaintop experience with the Great I Am, I expected an attempt at push-back from the unholy one. Well, it came with the strength of a hurricane. All I can do is hold on. Hold on to these five words, "I trust in you, Jesus."

While I understand that getting the snot kicked out of me is an opportunity to strengthen and demonstrate my faith in Jesus, it is not something I relish. I am, at heart, a wuss.

Then I read about the hundreds of people in Kenya who were just gunned down because they identified themselves as Christians. I am rightfully put in my place for my wussy-ness.

Oh Jesus, You died so I could live—not so I could live for myself but so I could live for you! To proclaim your glory and your grace! I humbly ask your forgiveness for cowering at the enemy, like the soldiers shaking in their armor before Goliath.

I ache to have the faith of David, to have the faith to boldly put it all on the line and claim victory in the name of the Living God! Thank you for working in me, for working on me, and for working through me.

David said to the Philistine, "You come against me with sword and spear and javelin, but I come against you in the name of the Lord Almighty, the God of the armies of Israel, whom you have defied. This day the Lord will deliver you into my hands, and I'll strike you down and cut off your head. This very day I will give the carcasses of the Philistine army to the birds and the wild animals, and the whole world will know that there is a God in Israel."
—1 Samuel 17:45–46 NIV

Fuge camp fugue

'Twas the night before Fuge
and all through our home,
excitement was building
as I wrote this poem.

"Where is my suitcase?
All this won't fit in!"
"You're not going for a month,"
I say with a grin.

The kids are all packed
and snug in their beds,
while visions of Mega Relay
dance in their heads.

I zip up their bags
and turn out the light.
Merry Fuge to all.
Don't let the bed bugs bite!

(Fuge is a Christian Youth Camp, held every summer across the
United States.)

This is the day that the LORD has made.
Let us rejoice and be glad in it.
—Psalm 118:24 NIV

Fork eew!

They tell me I stuck a fork in my sister's head when I was a little girl. No, she does not resemble a baked potato. She was quite beautiful and is to this day, despite the prong marks in her left temple. Konikoff legend has it that it all began on a dark and stormy night. I was in the top bunk bed. My older sister had just returned from a hospital stay, having had her appendix removed. My brothers describe the scene as chaotic. I apparently fell off the top bunk into my sister's arms. She, having fresh stitches in her abdomen, could no longer hold me and unceremoniously dumped me on the floor. This did not sit well with me. All night long I plotted my revenge and premeditated a breakfast table coup. Waiting for just the right moment, and just the right angle of entry, I made my move. Faking a stab at my pancakes, I doubled back and jabbed the fork in the sweet spot between her eyebrow and hairline. I believe my sister has forgiven me. Although, I never have been invited to breakfast …

You then, why do you judge your brother or sister?
Or why do you treat them with contempt? For we
will all stand before God's judgment seat.
—Romans 14:10 NIV

THE CRAZY OLD LADY
WHO LIVES UPSTAIRS

My oldest daughter has my back. She likes to say, "Mom, I don't just have your back, I got your circumference!" Man, I love that kid. There have been many times through our years together when she has proven her loyalty, but I choose to share with you now her premiere performance.

Who can resist freshly smoothed wet cement? Back in the summer of 1990, the city of Buffalo decided to tear up the sidewalk in front of my home. Upon repairing the damage, the workmen sectioned off the replaced sections with fresh cement. My eleven-year-old daughter was outside, playing with her friends, and I just so happened to be looking out the window as the workers packed up the truck and drove away. I felt a strange beckoning and a compulsion to go outside, much like I imagine the sailor's call to return to the sea, or a beagle to its feces. I walked toward the wet cement, as if in a trance. Looking up and down the street, my daughter and I caught each other's eye. She quickly busied herself with her friends, knowing her mom too well, and anticipating the humiliation of what was inevitably to come. The excitement grew inside of me as I searched the grass for the perfect tool. Plunging the stick into the cement, I fashioned the letters R K and the date. I was busy making history and failed to notice the workmen returning to the scene of my crime. Coming out of my haze, I ran in the house and locked the door! I ran to the open window just in time to hear one of the men ask my daughter if she knew who had defiled the new sidewalk. Without batting an eye, she said, "It's the crazy old lady who lives upstairs." Man, I love that kid.

God sets the lonely in families.
—Psalm 68:6a NIV

CHANCES ARE

I flew a plane last summer. I saw a Groupon for a flying lesson, my kids were out of town at camp, and I hadn't purposely placed my life in peril since some friends and I got a rental car stuck in the swamp at Ponce de Leon Park and were forced to climb up a tree and wait for two salivating crocodiles to lose interest and wander off. Well, I take that back. There was that time in the parking garage of my Honolulu apartment, when I sat in my little blue Fiat convertible for three hours, waiting for a banana spider the size of a Buick to crawl far enough away from the elevator for me to make a run for it.

My God, my rock, in whom I take refuge, my shield,
and the horn of my salvation, my stronghold and my
refuge, my Savior; you save me from violence.
—2 Samuel 22:3 NIV

NEVER TURN YOUR BACK ON A LOADED GLOCK

I remember getting that phone call you never want to get from the hospital emergency room, telling you to come right away because your daughter has been in a car accident. They wouldn't tell me if she was all right, so I panicked, jumped in the car, and floored it down Harris Boulevard. A police officer pulled me over. I had never been pulled over before, so I wasn't familiar with the etiquette. I jumped out of my car and ran up to the police car, arms flailing and mouth moving. The young officer, apparently startled at my maniacal display, shouted through the glass for me to get back in my car. I proceeded to explain that I was on my way to the hospital, not knowing if I would find my daughter dead or alive when I got there! He wasn't having any of my Mama Bear sass and got out of his vehicle while ordering me to take a seat in my car. Pure adrenaline and New York moxie came out of my mouth as I heard myself say, "Officer, I don't have time for this." Oh no she didn't!

Oh yes, she did. He pulled his gun, pointed it at me and repeated the order for me to take a seat in my car. I had never had a gun pointed at me before, so I think that accounted for my disregard as to the gravity of the situation. I told the officer that I was going to the hospital, he could follow me if he wanted to, but that, "I must be on my way." I turned and walked away from that loaded firearm. It was then that my mind allowed me to weigh the possible consequences of my defiance. Tomorrow's headline flashed through my mind, but I had already committed to this. I was all in. I made it to my car and to the hospital. My daughter was injured, but she healed quickly, and I never saw that officer again.

Kids, do not try this at home. I am a professional—professional idiot. That police officer was right to stop me. I was out of my mind and in no safe condition to drive. I thank him for not shooting me but wouldn't have blamed him if he had. I disobeyed the law and a direct order from a police officer. That was sixteen years ago. I hope the statute of limitations has run out by now!

The way of fools seems right to them,
but the wise listen to advice.
—Proverbs 12:15 NIV

Veiled Vanity

I make mistakes. I let people down. I hurt people. I make bad decisions that take me in the opposite direction from where I say I want to go. I give in to temptation and it happens *so quickly*. I go into damage control and minimize my errors and my culpability in situations. I resist change, yet I claim to desire it. I become defensive when emotionally threatened. I wonder if there will ever be a day when I will "get it right." Then I remember that Jesus Christ died to "get it right" for me.

When I realize that my never-ending, all-consuming, focus on how un-Jesus I am is still a focus on *me*, I am reminded of the futility of trying to save myself from myself. To drive home this debilitating self-centeredness, notice that I have used twenty-six personal pronouns so far! This is a "sin which so readily (deftly and cleverly) clings to and entangles us" (Hebrews 12:1 AMP).

Scripture clearly tells us to "fix our eyes on Jesus" (Hebrews 12:2 NIV). Scripture clearly shows us what happens when we shift our focus off of Jesus and "see the wind" (Matthew 14:30 NIV). Down, down, down we go.

Here's my radical suggestion. Replace every mirror in the house with a picture of Jesus, reminding us that it is Him we seek. May we then look only to, rely only on, and reflect only Him.

For those God foreknew he also predestined to be
conformed to the image of his Son, that he might be
the firstborn among many brothers and sisters.
—Romans 8:29 NIV

SINGLE MOMS, NOT SCHEMING SIRENS

A significant number of my clients are single moms. Upon hearing the same thing from a majority of them, and being a card-carrying member myself (yes, we have cards), I thought it may be of service to bring this issue forward. These incredible women all voice a similar disappointment concerning a lack of friends—not dates or romantic relationships, but friendships. Due to the demands on them and nervousness about their motives being misinterpreted, they often hesitate to approach others to initiate friendships. Ladies, not all single moms are out to steal your husbands or line you up as babysitters. Gentlemen, yes, fatherless kids could sure use good role models, but we are not looking for replacement daddies. We are looking for strong and lasting friendships—the kind we see reflected in your Facebook pictures of ladies beach retreat weekends, picnics, retail therapy sessions, and lunch trips. Most of these women are fascinating, strong, and loving souls. If they weren't my clients, I'd definitely be hanging with them!

I am not advocating for a "Take a Single Mom to Lunch Day" but for something much more genuine—a greater awareness of those wonderful, albeit weary, women who would make amazingly precious friends.

So speak encouraging words to one another. Build up hope so you'll all be together in this, no one left out, no one left behind. I know you're already doing this; just keep on doing it.
—1 Thessalonians 5:11b MSG

INTO EACH LIFE A LITTLE PAIN MUST FALL

If you have ever been there for others going through the experience of having a broken heart, you know that helpless feeling of wanting to take away their pain. You can listen, hold them, and keep the Kleenex coming. You can trust God, thank Him for removing a negative influence, and help pick up the pieces of a wounded spirit.

We all grieve loss; we all have pain. Remember that the gift of your presence can be like an umbrella in a storm. Walk alongside those you love. Offer a shoulder and an encouraging word of truth. Be the flashlight of faith during a time of temporary darkness, leading your loved one to the rock.

In this instance, the broken heart came as a result of a friend's return to drug use. If you know something, consider telling that person's loved ones then remember to extend grace as he or she reacts. That person may respond out of shock, denial, anger, embarrassment, fear, ignorance, or gratefulness. Regardless of the reaction, never hesitate to risk saving a life.

So the LORD spoke kind and comforting
words to the angel who talked with me.
—Zechariah 1:13 NIV

Family Force Night

Friday night at our house is affectionately referred to as Family Force Night. This is the night when the kids are obligated to spend the evening at home with Mom. What happens when two teenagers and an adult commit to "enjoying" each other's company for five solid hours? We are only limited by our imagination! Jell-O sculpting contests, our version of Project Runway with our dog as the model, sharing our favorite Vines, most annoying body noises (my son holds the crown), and making memories that will cause us to laugh out loud at inappropriate moments years from now. This is the stuff that families are made of. Well, ours is, anyway. I used to insist on holding technology-free weekends, but withdrawal symptoms became too strong for us all.

I encourage you to create and hold on to as much together time as you can. Let each memory add another color to your family rainbow, so that in the midst of the storms of life you will remember your blessings.

Children are a heritage from the Lord,
offspring a reward from him.
—Psalm 127:3 NIV

Saint not

I am no saint. Why should you listen to me? Oh, that's easy—because God has been using donkeys and sinners to teach us lessons about ourselves for thousands of years, and I qualify under both categories (Numbers 22:28 NIV). I would have to argue with the apostle Paul when he claimed to be the worst of all sinners (1 Timothy 1:15 NIV). I have broken every one of the commandments, ad nauseam. I'm not bragging or going for the championship belt, but I am confessing my desperate need of an awesome Savior.

I am one of God's many walking miracles, proving that He never gives up on us. I was thirty-six years old when I came to my senses and opened my eyes to the one I had been serving; and it wasn't God. I left a trail of emotional and relational destruction behind me to rival the path of a Merkava Mk.4 main battle tank. Choices I made directed the course of my life and altered the lives of my children. Thank you, Lord, for your promises of restoration and healing (Joel 2:25 NIV).

I once was blind, but now I have no excuse. I see and internally feel the consequences of my fickle allegiance. God still loves me, in the midst of my arrogance and my ignorance. He continues to mold me and make me into the image of Jesus. There were times He had to pry my fingers off of a desire or dream I'd been holding onto. I couldn't understand why I had to let them go (Job 1:21 NIV). I was sure I knew who I was and what I was here for. I was really good at justifying my mini-view of His plan, forgetting He is the architect. I would determine I knew what He wanted and run off in the wrong direction. Eventually, I learned that God doesn't need project managers; He wants servants, servants who choose to give our lives back to the one who gives us life. So if God sent His son to redeem me, the worst of sinners, there is a balm in Gilead waiting for you. Apply it liberally.

You alone are the Lord. You made the heavens, even the highest heavens, and all their starry host, the earth and all that is on it, the seas and all that is in them. You give life to everything, and the multitudes of heaven worship you.
—Nehemiah 9:6 NIV

LIFE IS LOUD

I have to be very intentional about finding quiet time. We live in a world with cities that never sleep, twenty-four-hour news channels, and all-night diners. Sometimes all the noise, stimulation, and vying for my sensual attention is deafening. My brain cannot process a television station with headlines scrolling across the top of the screen superimposed over news video and two rows of endless stock market reports and sports scores scrolling across the bottom. Sometimes my phone will ring, Facebook will ding, and Instant Messenger will bing all at the same time!

Just walking through the local mall is an experience in overstimulation—all the different smells coming from the food court and each individual store's choice of music, signature scent, and lighting. Then there are the kiosks in the walkway with the guerilla warfare assault salesforce and the teeming masses wandering around like shopping salmon, swimming upstream. If He leads me beside quiet waters to restore my soul, then this ain't it, and I need to get thee outdoors!

For God is not a God of disorder but of peace …
—1 Corinthians 14:33a NIV

LIFE IS FAST

I'm driving and listening to praise music, feeling very close to God and very loving toward my fellow commuters. As a way to extend a courtesy, I slow down to let someone in my lane. They accept my invitation but do not offer the conciliatory "wave of thanks," which I have come to expect as appropriate acknowledgment of my grand gesture. Oh how quickly my praise-filled thoughts turn to bitter disdain as I judge, ridicule, and label this ungrateful ingrate as "raca" from the protection of my car. The speed at which I lose my love for mankind makes me question how genuine it was to begin with! Time for a refresher.

Can both fresh water and salt water flow from the same spring?
—James 3:11 NIV

LIFE IS INTENSE

My oldest brother is a professional trumpet player. He was born to play the horn, and, man, can he play! When I went off to New York to pursue my music career, I lived with him until I could get my own place. He would practice his trumpet for hours every day. That trumpet never left his sight, let alone his hand. He had a special mute that he designed to place over the bell of the horn to muffle the sound so it wouldn't disturb the neighbors. It was an amazing device and allowed him to hone his screech chops without alerting the police. Where was Shark Tank when you could have cashed in on that mute, Ross?

This was midtown Manhattan in the late 1970s. Before my brother determined to eliminate all possible bug infestations by hermetically sealing up every crack and crevice in his apartment, there was an occasional visit from a New York City cockroach. I'm sure it came by to listen to the swinging jazz in Apartment H. On one particular day, my brother called me to witness something. I noticed an impressively large cockroach crawling through the hallway. My brother put the bell of his trumpet directly over that thing and hit a quadruple, triple C above high C—mute-free—and killed that beast with one literal blow. It sure was that sucker's last trumpet call!

In a moment, in the twinkling of an eye, at the last trumpet.
—1 Corinthians 15:52a ESV

LIFE IS RELENTLESS

The constant recycling from morning to evening, back to morning and back to evening, happens with no human intervention. It is completely beyond the reaches of our control. We can't start it, slow it down, or stop it. This was never made clearer to me than the day my father died. My mother, my daughter, and I were in the hospital room when the nurse said that Daddy's breathing indicated that he did not have long to live. The next sequence of events is forever etched in my mind. Daddy's breathing was very labored. Momma leaned over him and whispered, "It's okay, Eli; you can go." He literally took his final breath and exhaled with the unmistakable sound of eighty-two years of breathing in and breathing out coming to completion. Momma reached over to close his eyes. I remember being torn between whether to comfort my mother, who had just lost her husband of fifty years, or comfort my little girl, who had just lost her grandpa, the only man whose love she had ever known.

What followed was hospital routing procedure, and we eventually left the hospital for the last time. When we stepped outside, I was so angry at what I saw. Life continued to go on outside around us. We still had to scrape the ice off the car windshield, pay the parking attendant, and stop at all the red lights on the drive home. Life was pulling me, no, dragging me forward. I wanted it to stop for just a second, out of respect and reverence for what had just happened. But it didn't. It wouldn't.

I understand the necessity of life's seemingly cruel and relentless pull, forcing me to move forward. Life is, after all, for the living.

"For my thoughts are not your thoughts, neither are your ways my ways," declares the Lord. "As the heavens are higher than the earth, so are my ways higher than your ways and my thoughts than your thoughts."
—Isaiah 55:8–9 NIV

Rules for fools

If you have school-age children, you must be familiar with carpool lines. Next to watching golf on television, there is no greater waste of precious time. You plan to get there early so that you can queue up as close to the front as possible. That means getting in the line about an hour ahead of time. In reality, all we are doing when we use this logic is moving all that dead time from the back half to the front half of the wait. So, here you sit. In the winter, you are forced to keep the car running in order to stave off cryonic suspension. When the weather is warmer, you need the air conditioner on to prevent your children's post-traumatic stress at the sight of Mommy resembling a slice of crispy bacon, stuck to the black leather seat of the car.

Carpool lines can be humiliating. We all like to think we are superior wait-ers, prepared with our beverage, our book, tablet, or various and sundry activities. So smug, we have planned ahead to ensure optimum use of our time. We sneer and turn up our noses at the poor fool who failed to plan ahead and has fallen prey to the ultimate in carpool humiliation—falling asleep in line. Having experienced this myself, I can attest that there is no coming back from this branding. There you lay, seat back, warm spring day, snoozing and unaware of the flurry of activity taking place around you, actually taking place *because* of you: cars forced to back up and go around you and the eyes of everyone casting silent curses on you during your most vulnerable moment.

You are finally awakened from your innocent faux pas by the tap on your window from a distraught teacher, an occasional car horn, or an unkind and vitreous remark leveled at you from a frustrated parent.

Lest we ever forget that there are rules, protocol, and decorum even in the carpool line at preschool. Kindness and grace have been passed by and thought of as an obstacle to be steered around, an unnecessary deterrent to be avoided. Compassion and "there but for the grace of God go I" have taken a back seat (pun intended) to the throne of Freud's famous King Baby.

So, if you think you are standing firm,
be careful that you don't fall!
—1 Corinthians 10:12 NIV

Matzo madness

I wanted fried matzos. I didn't plan ahead, so I did not have the proper ingredients on hand to make them the usual way. I thought I could improvise a little. (I should have read my own writing about my cooking prowess.) I had the matzo crackers, the eggs, and butter, but I didn't have the purified water I like to use. Spotting a bottle of French vanilla creamer in the refrigerator door, I set out to make what I anticipated would be a similar, albeit somewhat sweeter version.

There's an expression my Southern friends use to describe something that is either very odd or very disturbing. These matzos were a "slap yo' momma" mess. Perhaps the extra sweetness and extra creaminess wouldn't have been so bad if I had thought to check the expiration date on the creamer. Perhaps the lumps in the creamer would have tipped of a more experienced chef. Perhaps I need to apply the following sage advice (pun intended) to a tried and true recipe. If it ain't broke, don't add rancid cream to it.

...for though the righteous fall seven times, they rise again, but the wicked stumble when calamity strikes.
—Proverbs 24:16 NIV

MORE OF YOU

More of you, less of me.
Fill me 'til I cease to be.
May it only be your face I see.
More of you, less of me.

More of you, less of me.
Calm the storms that rage in me.
Give me rest from all I strive to be.
More of you, less of me.

How hard I try to reach you.
How hard I try to please.
Constantly in motion,
But never on my knees.

All of you, none of me.
Help me seek you endlessly—
The Provider of the life I need.
All of you, none of me

He must become greater; I must become less.
—John 3:30 NIV

Whoa to Woe

I am a single mom and an only parent. Sometimes I really feel sorry for myself. It's usually when something goes wrong with the car or the house. You see, when I get this ginormous chip on my shoulder about how things "should" be, it blocks my view of how things actually are. The problem occurs in that passage of time between transitioning from my fantasy to reality. I fight it as long as I can and run the gamut of emotions until I am on the floor, exhausted, sobbing with snot in my hair and having spent every ounce of self-entitled bitterness I have been harboring. God stays with me the whole time, but like an addict on day five of opiate withdrawal, I have to go through it to get through it.

There are occasional tornadoes in North Carolina. This one was packed with lots of wind and lots of rain. Thunder and lightning filled the sky as my little ones and I waited it out from inside the house. We heard a loud crack and I looked out the window to see my beautiful one-hundred-year-old weeping willow tree, the centerpiece of my backyard, uprooted and laying across the top of my fence. Knowing that the tree was a goner and seeing that it was trying to take out the fence as its swan song, I ran outside, into the beast of the storm. There I stood, amid the cracking lightning, rolling thunder, and torrential rain. There I stood, all five foot two inches of me. There I stood, so filled with self-righteous indignation. *Really?* I thought. Now I have to single-handedly handle this too?

I channeled all my rage into trying to push the tree off of the fence to prevent the fence from being pulled down by the weight of the tree. Soaking wet, dodging lightning bolts, and yelling at God about the unfairness of the situation. I must have been a sight to behold. You know those stories about people being able to lift cars from the power of their adrenalin? Well, it wasn't happening for me that day. I reluctantly gave up trying to lift the giant tree off the fence. I screamed at God, and He answered me in shouts of thunder that shook the ground, as if to remind me with whom I was speaking.

When I finally screamed myself hoarse, I came back in the house to dry off. God made his point with me, but He also comforted me. He allowed me to be angry and express all the frustration, hurt, and disappointment I was feeling. I like to say that he and I had it out that day. I am grateful that my God allows me to react to my storms but lets me know He's in them with me. The next day two neighbors came by, kindly removed the tree and repaired my fence. Thank you, Lord.

Have you an arm like God and can you
thunder with a voice like his?
—Job 40:9 NIV

GOD'S GOT IT

Abraham walked up that hill, Isaac by his side.
Who'd have guessed that he'd be blessed and the sacrifice denied?
God's got it; yeah, God's got it.
No mistakes; He's got what it takes; God's got it.

Daniel saw those lions' jaws, and he heard that dinner bell.
His God knew that he would have a different tale to tell.
God's got it, yeah, God's got it.
No mistakes; He's got what it takes; God's got it.

Three young men about to burn for what they knew was true.
Almost toast, but God was close, and He came to their rescue.
God's got it; yeah, God's got it.
No mistakes; He's got what it takes; God's got it.

When it looks like all is lost and troubles cover you,
It all feels wrong, but before too long you'll change your point of
view.

God's got it; yeah, God's got it.
No mistakes; He's got what it takes; God's got it.

But Jesus looked at them and said, "With man this is impossible, but with God all things are possible."
—Matthew 19:26 ESV

A NIGHT TO REMEMBER

The story I am about to share is true; I was there, and I even have a hard time believing. Daddy was a musician. In the prime of his career he would play six nights a week. That meant Momma would be home alone with the four kids. He also owned and operated a dry cleaning business, so we had a truck—a Step Van truck. This wasn't a truck for the faint of heart. It had a manual transmission and not your standard H or your modern console stick. You had to know what you were doing to drive this baby. And this weren't no baby!

For out-of-town gigs, Daddy would have the musicians meet at the house, and everyone would drive to the job in one car. The musicians would park their cars across the street from the house, next to the big blue Step Van. On this particular dark and stormy night (there have been a few), Daddy and the band were off playing, my oldest sister was on a date, and my oldest brother had gotten a ride to a party. That left Momma at home with my other brother and me. The house phone rang (remember those days when it was a house phone?), and Momma said, "We have to pick up your brother from the party." Daddy had taken the station wagon, so that meant Momma would have to drive the Step Van (insert suspenseful music). She loaded us into the truck, which was tricky, because the musicians had parked too close to the Step Van, and it was impossible to squeeze inside from the driver's side. We all climbed in the passenger door. Momma sat there for a few minutes, trying to figure out how to maneuver this big fella. There were no side or rearview mirrors, no passenger seats, and no seatbelts. She mustered enough courage to start it up, and my brother and I cheered in celebration. Several minutes of ear piercing stripping of the gears followed, but Momma eventually found what she thought was first gear. It was reverse and we were all very surprised to be going backward, until she slammed on the brakes. It took about ten minutes for Momma to get the truck out from in between the parked cars and headed down the unlit road. We were all grateful that she did not smash into any of the parked cars.

We traveled in silence, as my anxious Momma had already warned us that if either of us so much as breathed too loudly we would be sorry. This silence allowed us all to concentrate on the road. We began to notice that approaching cars would honk their horns and swerve off the road as we passed by. We thought Momma was doing a good job of staying on her side of the road, so we didn't understand the drama on the other side of the road. After watching about ten cars drive off the road and career into the ditch, Momma broke the sound barrier by asking, "What is everyone's problem?" Momma turned her head to the left, glancing out the left side of the truck. I have never heard a noise come out of another human being to match what I heard at that moment. My brother and I ran up behind Momma and looked for ourselves. Momma had somehow hooked the drummer's Volkswagen Beetle to the left side of the truck and we were pulling it alongside of us down the road! We were taking up both lanes on this two-lane road, forcing each approaching driver to veer off into the ditch, as they could not see the attached vehicle until it was almost too late.

We had no choice but to continue this insane ride to pick up my brother. He was the hit of the party when Momma pulled up in the truck with the literal side car. We got the two vehicles home, parked them in the same spots, unhooked the Beetle, checked for scratches (none!), and called it a night—a night to remember.

Clean the slate, God, so we can start the day
fresh! Keep me from stupid sins.
—Psalm 19:12 MSG

ONLY LOVE

All my eyes have seen,
All my ears have heard,
Never once assured me of love.

Then I learned of one
Who had sent His son
As a ransom from
Up above.

There has never been,
Nor will ever be,
Such a sacrifice
Made for you and me.

On a cross of wood,
So misunderstood
By the world He died to free.

Only Love would go;
Only Love would know;
Only Love would go for me.

Greater love has no one than this: to lay
down one's life for one's friends.
—John 13:15 NIV

IRREVERENT REVERENCE

I was reading the Bible and thinking about the condition of the world. You don't mess around with God. Don't you just love the word "awesome"? There are at least thirty-five instances in which it appears in the Old Testament and it is used exclusively to describe God. Just like the word "love," "awesome" has been misused, and people have become desensitized to it as a powerful descriptor. "I love tacos," and "That playoff game was awesome" have cheapened both meaning and appropriate use. When we read of God's awesomeness, we, like Joshua, ought to fall on our faces in absolute reverence.

Israel has always been and will always be God's remnant. In these days of what I refer to as the Twenty-First Century Holocaust, both Christians and Jews are threatened with world annihilation. This is horrifying, and it is already happening. However, I am greatly encouraged when I read in Zephaniah 2:10–11 NIV.

> This is what they will get in return for their pride, for insulting and mocking the people of the LORD Almighty. The LORD will be awesome to them when he destroys all the gods of the earth. Distant nations will bow down to him, all of them in their own lands.

I am rocked to the core and shudder every time I am reminded of this verse from Hebrews 10:31 NIV: "It is a dreadful thing to fall into the hands of the living God."

Let us not become like the ones we oppose. God calls on us to love our enemies and to pray for them. I have no doubt we are praying, but are we praying for our enemies? Foreign soil or next door. Let's get on our knees and submit ourselves in prayer to intercede for those who desire to kill us. What a way to worship; what a way to witness to the world. Jesus was sentenced to crucifixion as the crowd desired to kill Him. He gave up His life as the ultimate sacrifice to save ours. He prayed for his persecutors as He hung on that cross.

But God demonstrates his own love for us in this:
While we were still sinners, Christ died for us.
—Romans 5:8 NIV

DOG IS MORE THAN GOD
SPELLED BACKWARDS

Last week I worked with a client as he grieved the sudden loss of his beloved dog. So much emotion and companionship existed in that relationship. I will always have a dog. I warned my kids that when I die, someone will have to come and let the dog out. There is no substitute for doggie love. Having failed miserably at long-term human interaction, I have built a lifetime of solid relationships with my canine counterparts. The unconditional love I get from my dog is the closest thing, aside from God's grace and forgiveness, that I have ever received on this earth. My dog doesn't care if I have gotten so fat that I can no longer bend over to clip my toenails. He doesn't complain if I binge watch old *Moonlighting* episodes. He is by my side when I am sick, and he knows when I'm sad, curling up very close to me and doing his lean-against-me-thing that I love so much!

No matter how many times I leave the house, he is always ecstatic upon my return, practically knocking me over with the wind velocity from his tail. He greets me the same way, whether I've had a bad day and need a soft place to land, or whether I've been the bully to someone else and need to feel pure unconditional love. Knowing that I am loved and accepted helps me to risk being vulnerable and taking that fearless moral inventory. That acceptance helps me to lay it all out there, finally looking at what God has been waiting for me to surrender to Him.

My God has a love for me that is so strong. Just the thought of it knocks me to my knees. My God holds me in His tender and gracious embrace as He pulls the thorns of bitterness and prideful arrogance from my heart. He is more than by my side every moment of my life. He is the provider of my next moment.

When I feel beat down by the world's impossible standards, He reminds me of who I truly am. When I feel ashamed of the way I have behaved, He gently educates me and reminds me of my worth in His eyes.

Lord, thank you for your love and for the most intimate of blessings in the form of unconditional love and acceptance from my dog. Thank you for giving me this as I work out my salvation with fear and trembling.

…who comforts us in all our troubles, so that
we can comfort those in any trouble with the
comfort we ourselves receive from God.
—2 Corinthians 1:4 NIV

BLUEBERRIES OF THE SPIRIT

I don't typically have a "bad day." I believe that a bad day is an attitude choice, and that anything can be turned around with a change in perspective. This morning, through a series of unfortunate circumstances, I succumbed to my first bad day. One thing after another went wrong, held me up, didn't work, got lost, dropped, and broke. Rushing around like a head with its chicken cut off (as Momma used to say), I dropped the quart of blueberries. That crazy-making plastic container popped open, and berries cascaded all over the floor. At least a hundred plump, violet anti-oxidants went everywhere! I stared at the mess and verbally beat myself up for being such a cotton-headed ninny muggings.

Then it happened. As I got down to gather up the berries, I was instantly brought to the realization that I was on my knees. It was the first time this morning that I had been on my knees. God did what was necessary to get me where I needed to be all along! From this physical position of surrender, I was emotionally and spiritually realigned. I listened and talked with my heavenly Father, and we retrieved the fruit together. I was so aware of His presence right there with me. He calmed my spirit and reminded me that I am His. One blueberry at a time, my mood was lifted and my spirit renewed. I don't know if I will ever look at blueberries in the same way. Thank you, Lord, for this lesson on the power that fruit can have on my spirit.

But the fruit of the Spirit is love, joy, peace, forbearance, kindness, goodness, faithfulness, gentleness and self-control. Against such things there is no law.
—Galatians 5:22–23 NIV

As if I Never Sang for My Father

I used to be a jazz and blues singer—stories for another book, I promise. I was driving home from my day job on a Wednesday night, and traffic was holding me up. I was scheduled to sing a solo in the Wednesday night service at my church, so I was pressed for time to get home, eat, and make it up to church in time for the sound check. My mind was preparing for the song, running the lyrics, and working out piano parts in my mind. The traffic light turned green, but the line of cars I was in did not budge. I looked ahead and saw drivers pulling around a stalled vehicle in our lane. People were beeping and racing their engines as they figuratively spit on the person who had the audacity to break down in front of them.

And then it was my turn to pull around that car, shoot the driver a look of disgust, and spin my tires at him in a self-righteous display. Not only did I participate in all of that, I also caught myself murmuring, "Get out of my way; I'm going to be late. I gotta go sing for God." As soon as the words left my self-absorbed lips, I was flattened by the swift and steadfast conviction of my Savior. Worse than the travelers who crossed to the other side of the road in the story of the Good Samaritan, I continued to church and made my offering of song to the Lord, an offering I am sure was empty and unacceptable to Him. He did, however, continue to work on me and has since enabled me to be part of the solution to a brother or sister in need.

Some of us get it right away, and some of us need our heads held in the cosmic toilet bowl. I don't look forward to those "swirlies," but they never fail to teach me the lesson I need to learn.

"Which of these three do you think was a neighbor to the man who fell into the hands of robbers?" The expert in the law replied, "The one who had mercy on him." Jesus told him, "Go and do likewise."
—Luke 10:36–37 NIV

Time out

So powerless. Here I sit, locked out. Keys and purse on the other side of the locked office door. I just stepped outside to put something in my car, and the office door closed and locked behind me. I have my phone, and anyone who would have a key has been called and is not answering. Tried all windows, credit card in door trick, brute force, and continued prayers for door to divinely and graciously unlock itself. Even my car keys are on the other side of that door, so I'm forced to stay here—forced to face this situation. Hardest of all, I'm forced to accept this situation.

After the adult temper tantrum, I have no choice but to sit quietly. In the stillness, in the lack of physical activity, my mind must adjust and slow down. I hear birds chirping and see the wind blowing through the trees. I feel the sun warming my skin. It is a gloriously beautiful morning, whether or not I choose to acknowledge it. My breathing slows down, and it is sinking in that there is absolutely nothing I can do but wait.

It has now been over four hours. I could break the glass and get in that way, but then I would have to arrange to replace the glass quickly. Right now all my money is riding on the janitor. He usually shows up to clean the bathrooms on Saturday afternoons. Please let this not be a day when he decides to stay home. Did I mention that I could sure use a restroom right now? Five hours and counting.

He showed up, opened the door for me, and the day proceeded as though nothing had ever happened. But something did happen to me. God put me in time out. He made me cease striving and know that He is God. He does that to us sometimes. I'm glad mine was just a time out. I know of others who have had it much harder when He needed to get their attention.

Be still and know that I am God.
—Psalm 46:10 NIV

Southern Fried

You can take the girl out of New York, but you can't take New York out of the girl! When my daughter and I first moved to North Carolina she was a junior in high school. Yep, and she's still not talking to me for that! We had a lot of adjusting to do. The first few weeks were a bit rough. I hadn't had enough time to get around to changing the license plates on my Wrangler and we were waiting at a signal when someone decided to welcome us to the South by yelling, "Yankee go home." Thank you and God bless! My daughter would come home from school in tears because the French teacher's heavy southern drawl made it nearly impossible for her to understand a word he was saying. I remember the moving truck pulling away and all the neighbors gathering around the snow blower, in awe and wonder about this strange contraption.

Perhaps the biggest shock for me was experiencing what is known around these-here-parts as barbecue. Where I come from, barbecue was a piece of chicken or beef with a lot of very sticky, very red sauce on it. To my horror, what I experienced in the South was a pile of tan strings, resembling old rubber bands, drenched in a clear liquid smelling of vinegar. I understand this is quite a treat around here, but to this Yankee, it has earned the name "barf-a-que."

Oh, but now that we have been here for several years, there are a few things that have grown on me. Back in New York, tea was hot and came in a cup. Now I am a sold-out soldier for sweet tea, church on Wednesday nights, the NASCAR All-Star race in May, Southern potato salad, and banana pudding. Do I even need to say any more than Chick-Fil-A?

The South has softened me quite a bit, and I like that. You say "Hey" to one another when you greet people. If you said "Hey" to someone in New York, they'd think you were looking for a fight. We actually listen to a country song once in a while, and I heard myself drop the "Y" bomb a few times—y'all. Thank you for accepting this reluctant refugee into your neck of the woods. (But I still like Dunkin' Donuts better than Krispy Kreme.)

I praise you because I am fearfully and wonderfully made;
your works are wonderful, I know that full well.
—Psalm 139:14 NIV

TEXT MISSILES

A teenage girl is hurting tonight – aching, because her boyfriend suddenly texted her that he doesn't want to see her anymore. The short text is sent, out of the blue, as he is on route for a week-long vacation with his family. He is hundreds of miles away. With a clear conscience, he can now enjoy his vacation.

Back home, she is heartbroken, blindsided, and desperately trying to figure out what she did wrong. With just a few clicks he hits 'send' and, in a remote location, a text missile of devastation is launched with nuclear proportions.

Disaster Recovery Teams are called to the scene in the form of Jesus, Mom, sister, brother, brother-in-law, best friends, teammates, church friends, work friends, overseas travel friends, retail therapy, various food groups, fuzzy blankets, and time.

Words are so powerful. Use them wisely.

There is one whose rash words are like sword thrusts,
but the tongue of the wise brings healing.
—Proverbs 12:18 NIV

It's all a blur

I see clients all day and don't have time to eat. I try to stay away from processed foods, so there isn't much I can store in my desk that will keep fresh all day. I usually end up not eating until I get home, and this used to cause a problem for me. By the time I would get home, I was ravenous. What happened next was a blur, but family members told me it resembled a shark feeding frenzy. It took all of about ten minutes, but the collateral damage lasted far longer. Food flying through the air, bags and boxes torn open and thrown to the floor, handfuls of this and that shoved into my mouth. Then it was over and there I lay, licking my chops and groaning from nausea. Aside from destroying any chance of having a good meal, the emotional avalanche buried me in guilt and shame.

When I was in middle school, we had a Scottish terrier named Rudy McTavish McDuff. We called him Duffy. One day, Momma had left out a pound of butter on the shelf to soften. When we got home from an errand, there lay Duffy on his side on the floor. Beside him was the butter wrapper, only the butter wrapper. He had consumed the entire pound of butter. He just laid there, on his side, licking his chops nonstop, in a trance. It was pitiful. That is how I felt after one of my feeding frenzies.

I have worked through all that and now have a non-adversarial relationship with food. The theme song from *Jaws*, however, does make me hungry ….

For God gave us a spirit not of fear, but of
power and love and self-control.
—2 Timothy 1:7 ESV

WHEN YOUR FOOT'S IN YOUR MOUTH, IT'S HARD NOT TO TRIP OVER YOUR TONGUE

I have a big mouth—big enough to fit both feet. Are you following me? My children cringe when they are out in public with me, because I love to talk to people. For me, having to wait in a line is an opportunity to hear some great stories, see people smile, and make the day better for somebody. I believe God has allowed us to be where we are at any given time and that we have an opportunity, even a responsibility, to make the most out of it for His glory.

Now that I am older, I care much less about what other people think of me. This is not necessarily a good thing, as it contributes to dismantling the verbal filter that acts as a speed bump between passivity and public humiliation.

There was that time I was approaching a man walking toward me from down a long hallway. It was late October, so I assumed he was feeling festive. Thinking I was in on his joke, I called out to him, "Hey, nice fake nose and glasses!" Anticipating a happy nod from him for my astute acknowledgment of his Halloween attire, I was horrified upon closer examination to discover he was not wearing any.

Or the time I tried to make small talk with the cashier at the grocery store, thinking he was using his name tag to be funny. I remarked, "That's pretty funny, making a statement by putting 'As If' for your name!" Once again, I was humbled to hear him quietly respond that his name was Asif.

I could deceive myself by saying that I'm just too hip for the room. Truth be told, it's very hard to walk and talk with both feet in your mouth.

"Remember to say not only the right thing in the right place, but far more difficult still to leave unsaid the wrong thing at the tempting moment".

—Benjamin Franklin

Even fools are thought wise if they keep silent,
and discerning if they hold their tongues.
—Proverbs 17:28 NIV

JUST DESSERTS

We went to a new restaurant tonight. It came highly recommended as having a famous dessert. That's enough of a recommendation for us. We are suckers for a good dessert. General consensus was that the food was a six; the service was a seven; there was no atmosphere, but the dessert lived up to its hype. Like true dessertaholics, we will return to sample the other four deliciously described offerings.

Food makes us happy. Dessert makes us very happy. In a world with so much fear, violence, uncertainty, and anxiety, it is refreshing to guiltlessly share a gooey confection with my kids. And they serve it on one plate, so it becomes a real family event! Hey, I am all about eating healthy, clean, and avoiding food additives. However, in moderation, let's not forget to enjoy these moments of pure culinary pleasure. You just don't get the same reaction sharing a bowl of hummus.

Go, eat your food with gladness, and drink your wine with a joyful heart, for God has already approved what you do.
—Ecclesiastes 9:7 NIV

NARCISSISTIC NOMENCLATURE—I NOW PRONOUNCE YOU TURKEY ON RYE

People are doing a lot of changing these days. They are attempting to change history by omitting actual events from history books in an effort to manipulate a new generation. They are changing meanings and definitions of words, not just to define new practices but to destroy the meaning of the original definition. I believe there is an ulterior motive here. If you want to do something different, call it something different. Why do something different and insist on calling it by the same name as something else, unless you are trying to force a change to its meaning?

If you want to make a sandwich with ham and cheese, call it a ham and cheese sandwich. Don't insist on calling it turkey on rye. Why would you want to call it turkey on rye unless you were trying to permanently change the meaning of turkey on rye to suit your tastes? Why can't you have your ham and cheese and let me have my turkey on rye? When I state that ham and cheese is not turkey on rye, and that I believe turkey on rye is actually turkey on rye, I am labeled a hater. You don't have to like my turkey on rye, and I don't have to like your ham and cheese, but you don't have to take away my turkey on rye in order to have your ham and cheese.

This mystery is profound, and I am saying
that it refers to Christ and the church.
—Ephesians 5:32 ESV

Enough already with the rubbing!

I'll never understand what the attraction is with getting a massage. All my clients love them; family members love them; I recommend them for my clients; and some of my best friends are massage therapists. So, it must be me. I used to joke and say that it has taken me half a century to build up all this physical tension, and I'm not giving it up for anyone! That may be a twisted excuse, but here's what I have to say, after having my first massage a few weeks ago. Eh. They assigned me to a male. He was very nice, not creepy, but I knew there was no way I would be able to relax with some guy rubbing his hands all over my flabby body. So I lay there, more than half-naked, wishing it would be over. He was a perfect gentleman, and I'm sure he did an excellent job with the uptight old lady on the table. "Oh, you were just nervous because it was your first time," everyone told me.

So, at the urging of my daughter, I went again, to a different massage therapist this time. I felt disloyal, like a cheating spouse, but the receptionist assured me this was not taboo. God bless this one; she worked hard for the money! Eh. By this time we have a one-year contract, so I must endure this failure-to-respond label for another two seasons. "Try another type of massage," they suggested.

I tried again. Having cheated before on the first masseuse, my heart was now hardened, and I engaged with a third. This masseuse was also very good, spent a lot of time on me, did the whole hot stones thing, aromatherapy, and meditative music—the whole shebang. There were actually moments during the grueling process when I wanted to scream, "Stop it! Enough already with the rubbing!" I have now determined that not only don't I enjoy it,

I actually loathe it. I felt guilty after this last over-the-top massage to beat all massages. So, aside from tipping her enough to put her children through college, I told her how wonderful it was. I am an encourager by nature.

For me, it was too much touching. An hour and a half of rubbing and rubbing and kneading and kneading. If I were a ball of yeast I'd have risen into a phenomenal loaf of bread. But I am just a flabby old lady. I guess you could say the whole thing just rubs me the wrong way!

Then he put his hands on her, and immediately
she straightened up and praised God.
—Luke 13:13 NIV

WHAT GOOD IS SITTING ALONE IN YOUR ROOM?

Momma tried very hard to give us all something that resembled a normal childhood. Daddy had two jobs, worked all the time, and that left Momma home to entertain the four of us. On Sundays, we would pack up the enormous metal cooler and head to Sherkston Beach. Pepsi in bottles, real butter, bagels, and corned beef. Daddy would sleep in the car while Momma and the kids would spend the entire day in the surf and the sand. The older kids got to go off and wander down the road to a place called the quarry. It was filled with water and had a diving platform so high that it was a rite of passage for any sixteen-year-old. You weren't allowed in the quarry unless you were at least sixteen. I never got to go, as we stopped these beach trips long before my sixteenth birthday. But my brothers and sisters would tell me stories. I would be back at the beach making sand castles with my pail and shovel, and my siblings would be having teenage kicks at the quarry. Rumor had it that there were dead bodies in that water.

On Saturdays, Momma would load us in the car and take us on adventures. I miss both her and her enthusiasm so much now, but at the time we all hated these excursions. She would take us to private zoos, to visit the canals and locks of Lake Erie, for train rides on the Lackawanna Railroad, and to various shrines and tourist attractions throughout New York. One outing, however, literally goes down in history. I don't know if she even knew how monumental this trip would be. In 1969, a research project was taking place to measure the erosion rate of Niagara Falls. Momma heard that the water had been diverted away and that people could actually walk across Niagara Falls. We did, and it was amazing! It was all rocks. Safety standards weren't like they are now, so you could walk right up to the edge and look down!

My daddy may have been the famous one, but my momma was something. She was someone who honestly "lived until she died." Even into her eighties, she rode her bike, belted out show tunes, and kicked up her heels doing what she loved. Hey, Momma, you got your wish. You got to go like Elsie!

I have come so that they may have life; life in its fullest.
—John 10:10b NIV

THE LITTLE EGG (BASED ON PROVERBS 3:5–6 NIV)

Once upon a time there was a Little Egg lying on the ground. The Little Egg wondered where he came from and how he got there. One moment, the Little Egg had decided that he must have always been there. The next moment, the Little Egg worried that he must have come from somewhere, but he didn't know where. Someone must have made him and put him in that spot on the ground, but he didn't know who. There were also times when he despaired that he was a mistake and that there was no reason for him to be there. So he became afraid.

Several days went by. The Little Egg was very uncomfortable and began stretching from the inside. He began pushing and moving around. Tiny cracks appeared in various places all over the shell of the Little Egg. One crack in particular was big enough for the Little Egg to peek out of. The once dark and closed shell now had light streaming in from where the crack split, and so the warmth of the sun could shine through. Every so often a breeze would blow and the Little Egg could smell the lilacs and hyacinths from nearby. The Little Egg's favorite smell was from the soft bed of spearmint growing all around and underneath him.

Each day the cracks became bigger and bigger, and the Little Egg could eventually see out of the shell—not very far, but a few feet in either direction. The Little Egg could finally see the brilliant colors of the flowers he had been smelling for so long. "Oh, how beautiful," thought the Little Egg! And the Little Egg had determined that the whole world must be just as beautiful as what he could see from inside his shell. He made friends with the worms and the creatures who lived around him.

On a particularly sunny day, the Little Egg was peering out of the crack and saw a bird swoop down from the sky, pull a worm out of the soil, and fly away with it in his mouth! "Oh, how dreadful," thought the Little Egg! And the Little Egg was so upset that he had determined that the whole world must be just as dreadful as what he could see from inside his shell. He made up his mind not to look out of the shell anymore. He felt very sad and alone, and he cried himself to sleep.

A large piece of the shell was so cracked and weakened that it looked as though it was about to fall off. The Little Egg held that piece in place with all of his might! He determined that he needed that piece of the shell. He did not want to lose his dark and closed shell. He was angry that he was becoming so big and that his shell was no longer comfortable for him. He began to worry about what was happening to him. Even as he fought to keep the piece in place, he knew that he couldn't stay in there for much longer, as he was becoming too big to remain inside. He had outgrown his shell. The Little Egg was very discouraged and blamed himself for breaking his shell.

But you see, the Little Egg had not just appeared out of nowhere. The Little Egg was indeed made. He was made with great intention, with great attention, and with great affection. He was not a mistake, and he was never, ever alone. He was made to come out of that shell and see much more than just a few feet on either side of the cracks he had been looking out of for so long.

The one who made the Little Egg appeared to him and explained that the Little Egg was not responsible for the cracks in the shell. The one who made the Little Egg was the one who carefully cracked open the shell, bit by bit. The one who made the Little Egg was the one who allowed him to feel the warmth of the sunlight, smell the fragrance of the beautiful flowers, rest in the softness of the spearmint, gaze at the brilliant colors all around him, and enjoy the love and friendship of the other creatures. The one who made him also allowed him to see the bird and the worm and was with the Little Egg while he cried, holding him gently while he slept.

The Little Egg came to trust the one who made him. He found that the world was so much more than what he had determined from his view inside of his shell. He stayed close to the one who made him, enjoying the warmth of the sunlight, the smell of the flowers, the softness of the spearmint, the brilliance of all the colors, and the love he received from all the other creatures. But best of all, he grew to trust and depend upon the love of the one who made him. He realized that once he trusted in the one who created him, cared for him, and loved him the most, he had no reason to ever be afraid again.

Trust in the LORD with your whole heart and lean
not on your own understanding. In all your ways
acknowledge him and he will direct your paths.
—Proverbs 3:5–6 NIV

Here he comes to save the day

When I was a little girl, I would wait by my bedroom window for Mighty Mouse to fly in and save the day. He never came. I would hear Captain Kangaroo tell me it was time to wake up Grandfather Clock, and I would say, "Good morning, Grandfather," and always be amazed that he heard me! I hated having to watch *The Wizard of Oz* every year, because the flying monkeys scared me. I was afraid a lot when I was little. There were a few things to be afraid of, back then. We had to practice air raid drills in kindergarten. We would be told to place our hands over our heads and get under our desks. We would practice going down in the basement of the school to hide in the fallout shelter. I remember staring at all the canned goods and wondering how long you could live there. We watched our teachers and parents cry when President Kennedy was shot. My parents received a phone call from someone saying he had kidnapped my sister, and I watched them go through the agony of those hours until she was located. My brothers told me that the gigantic steel power structures were monsters called Raybars and that they were coming to eat me. And there were a few other very significant events that taught me that life was not safe.

To help me deal with all that fear, I used to sing and dance up and down the driveway, making up elaborate musical productions. Even at the age of six, I knew I was going to be a star. I knew one day I would show that fear who was boss! A lot has happened along the way. There were times when I was a star and times when I wasn't. Times when I knew what I was doing and times when I didn't. Times when I thought I was in love and times when I realized I wasn't. I still look up and wish my hero would fly in my window and save the day, but then I remember that he already has. My real hero, my Savior Jesus Christ, has already saved the day and all of eternity for us if we recognize our desperate need for Him. If we admit we are sinners and that we need His gift of salvation from the wages of sin, then we can have eternal life with Him in heaven after we die.

I did that at thirty-six years old. After many bad choices, I handed the reins of my life over to God. God never stopped waiting for me to see who He is, who I truly am, and what He did for me because He loves me. He feels the same way about you. Tell God you know that you are a sinner and that you need the Savior, Jesus Christ. Confess with your mouth, and believe in your heart that Jesus is Lord, and you will be saved and receive eternal life with God.

For all have sinned and come short of the glory of God.
—Romans 3:23 NIV

For the wages of sin is death, but the gift of God
is eternal life through Jesus Christ our Lord.
—Romans 6:23 NIV

But God demonstrates his own love toward us, in that
while we were still sinners, Christ died for us.
—Romans 5:6 NIV

If you confess with your mouth Jesus as Lord,
and believe in your heart that God raised
him from the dead, you will be saved.
—Romans 10:9 NIV

For everyone who calls on the name of the Lord will be saved.
—Romans 10:13 NIV

From Toddler Excitement to Teenage Angst

I love my teenagers. I love seeing them taking responsibility for the choices they are making. It is thrilling to watch them use their wings to fly outside the nest and rewarding to listen to them talk about what they discovered when they return home. But I miss the smiles, hugs, and kisses that came every morning upon awakening. I miss their joy and excitement at just being given another day to experience. When they were little, it was all about the now—the very moment they were in. Look at those fireworks! Taste those snowflakes! Feel that slimy toad! Smell those cookies baking! Hear that ice cream truck! These days it's all about the next moment, what's coming up, what we have planned for later, for this weekend, and for after graduation. They worry about the exam, the prom, the game, the group chat, the scale, and the mirror. I ran across the once favorite stuffed animal of my youngest. I took it to him, and there was a moment of recognition and a warm smile before he handed it back to me and rushed out the door.

Sometimes I catch myself doing that with God. I get so caught up in anticipation or dread over the next moment. When God speaks, touches my heart, or hands me a reminder of our relationship, I do stop and acknowledge Him. But far too often these days, there is a moment of recognition and a warm smile before I rush out the door. Keep me close, Lord Jesus.

But I have this against you, that you have left your first love.
—Revelation 2:4 NASB

Let us examine and probe our ways, and
let us return to the LORD.
—Lamentations 3:40 NIV

JESUS CHRIST
THE
REALITY CHECK
THAT WILL NEVER
BOUNCE

Printed in the United States
By Bookmasters